CRIME SCIENCE

COLD CASES

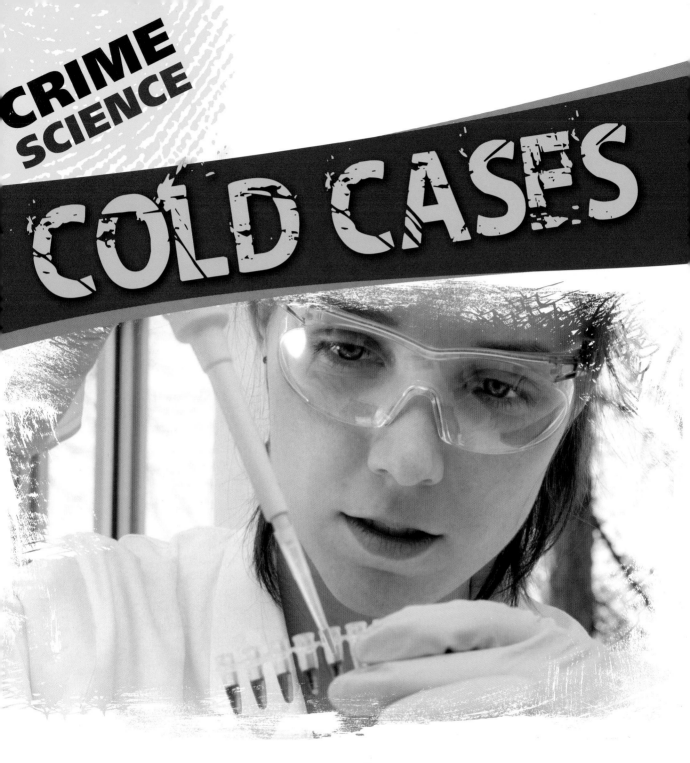

Matt Anniss

Gareth Stevens
Publishing

Please visit our website, www.garethstevens.com. For a free color catalog of all our high-quality books, call toll free 1-800-542-2595 or fax 1-877-542-2596.

Library of Congress Cataloging-in-Publication Data

Anniss, Matt.
Cold cases / by Matt Anniss.
  p. cm. — (Crime science)
Includes index.
ISBN 978-1-4339-9477-7 (pbk.)
ISBN 978-1-4339-9478-4 (6-pack)
ISBN 978-1-4339-9476-0 (library binding)
1. Cold cases (Criminal investigation) — Juvenile literature. 2. Murder — Investigation — Juvenile literature. I. Anniss, Matt. II. Title.
HV6515.A56 2014
363.25—dc23

First Edition

Published in 2014 by
Gareth Stevens Publishing
111 East 14th Street, Suite 349
New York, NY 10003

© 2014 Gareth Stevens Publishing

Produced by Calcium, www.calciumcreative.co.uk
Designed by Keith Williams and Paul Myerscough
Edited by Sarah Eason and Jennifer Sanderson

Photo credits: Cover: Shutterstock: Bork. Inside: Dreamstime: Bruce2 19, Moth 36, Pavla 40, Tossi66 34; Shutterstock: 18percentgrey 5b, Ad Oculos 26, Anneka 13, Anyaivanova 1, 11, 37, Kevin L Chesson 44, 45, Convit 24, Corepics VOF 4, Fer Gregory 42, Steve Heap 35, Eddies Images 22, 29b, Edw 8, Goodluz 17, Fisun Ivan 10, Junial Enterprises 39, Ragne Kabanova 27, Peter Kim 7, 16, Georgios Kollidas 41, Vasiliy Koval 43, Mikeledray 6, 25, Mishella 14, Nobeastsofierce 30, Olivier 18, Photomak 21, Nikita G. Sidorov 33, Leah-Anne Thompson 5t, 12, 15, 20, 23, 29t, 32, Wavebreakmedia 28, Pan Xunbin 31, Lisa F. Young 38; Wikimedia Commons: Fallout boy 9t, Joe Mabel 9b.

Printed in the United States of America

CPSIA compliance information: Batch #CS13GS: For further information contact Gareth Stevens, New York, New York at 1-800-542-2595.

CRIME SCIENCE

CONTENTS

COLD CASES

There are many crimes that cannot be solved. These "cold cases" may remain unsolved for years, even indefinitely, but thanks to major advances in science, many are reopened and solved every year.

Dusty Files

When detectives are investigating a criminal case, if it cannot be solved, it is kept "on file." If new evidence is found, or new techniques are developed that can then be used to retest existing evidence, the case will be reopened.

New Techniques

In recent years, many cold cases have been reopened and evidence has been reexamined using new, modern crime-science techniques. These techniques have helped to convict many criminals for crimes they committed years ago.

Before a case is classified as "cold," every shred of evidence is studied and tested to find vital clues.

The Role of Crime Science

Science is vital to the teams trying to crack cold cases. There are many forensic-science techniques that can be used to reexamine old evidence, from carefully examining bullets found at the crime scene to magnifying old pictures using computer software. Not all of these will get results in every case, so there are many cold cases still unsolved. However, detectives stand a much greater chance of solving crime mysteries thanks to cutting-edge forensic-science techniques.

Crime-scene evidence must be carefully handled and kept in sterile bags.

Powerful microscopes make it now possible to find new clues about past crimes buried deep in old clothing, blood samples, and even human hairs.

BACK IN THE LAB

Many police forces employ teams of forensic scientists to work exclusively on cold cases. Their job is to review all the evidence on file and, where appropriate, carry out new tests in the police laboratory using modern techniques. This could include looking for traces of clothing fibers or human skin, examining weapons under a microscope, and using computer software to figure out the exact angle a bullet entered a victim's body.

CHAPTER ONE
WHEN CASES GO COLD

Do not be fooled by the ease at which detectives on television solve crimes. Many criminal cases, particularly violent ones such as murders, can be incredibly complicated. Because of this, the number of cold cases is added to every year.

Outdated Methods

Many cold cases that are reopened today are historic, meaning that they happened many years ago. The idea of using forensic-science techniques to crack crimes is a new development. Years ago, detectives had very few forensic-science methods at their disposal. Instead, they had to rely on traditional methods of police work, such as interviewing witnesses, taking crime-scene photographs, and searching for evidence.

Lack of Evidence

In some cases, traditional police methods were enough to crack the case. However, there were plenty of times when these techniques did not deliver results. For example, police still have unsolved murder cases on file that went cold 40 years ago due to a lack of strong evidence. Without the scientific techniques to examine the tiniest piece of evidence, detectives had little to go on in many cases.

Modern-day crime scenes are sealed off to try to retain vital forensic evidence that could help solve the crime.

SHERIFF'S LINE DO NOT

Fingerprint Analysis

In the past, forensic science techniques were limited. One of the most widely used was fingerprint analysis. Everyone's fingerprints are different, so fingerprint analysis is a useful tool. However, there are problems with the system. For example, a fingerprint alone is not proof of guilt, and many criminals wear gloves to avoid detection.

The fingerprints of known criminals are stored on a database that can be accessed by the police.

CRACKED

If you examine the tips of your fingers, you will notice patterns of lines and rings, called friction ridges. Every person's friction ridges are slightly different, so their fingerprints are different. When examining a crime scene, detectives look for marks made by these ridges on surfaces such as glasses, tables, and windows. These marks may have been made in the process of committing the crime and could help to identify the criminal.

GENUINE MYSTERIES

Due to a lack of what police call "tangible" evidence or witnesses, some crimes are genuine mysteries. These are the most difficult to solve, especially those that are historic. Some of the world's most famous cold cases fall into this group.

Many Cold Cases

According to the Center for the Resolution of Unsolved Crimes, in the last 30 years there have been hundreds of thousands of violent crimes in the United States that remain on file as cold cases. The Center estimates that since 1980, there have been around 185,000 unsolved murder cases. Some of these are unsuitable for reexamination using modern scientific techniques. Of those that are, only a fraction will ever be solved.

Cold cases can only be solved if crime-scene investigators log, note, and retain every piece of evidence so that it can be examined again.

Mysterious Killer

Even high-profile cases involving multiple homicides can remain unsolved. One of the most famous examples is that of the "Zodiac Killer," who murdered at least four women in California between 1968 and 1970. Despite the police receiving letters from the killer, various tip-offs, and huge interest from the public, the Zodiac Killer has never been identified. It is unlikely he will ever be caught, even though the California Department of Justice has kept the case open for more than 40 years.

The "Zodiac Killer" gave away few clues as to his identity, other than a logo he used to sign his letters.

The "Green River Killer" earned his nickname after dumping his victims' bodies in the Green River.

REAL-LIFE CASE

In 2001, one of the most notorious serial killers was caught thanks to modern forensic techniques. Gary Ridgway, nicknamed the "Green River Killer," murdered at least 49 women during the 1980s and 1990s. Although he managed to avoid detection, the police took hair and saliva (spit) samples from Ridgway in 1987 when they questioned him about another crime. In 2001, these samples were tested with new DNA technology and found to match samples found on the bodies of four of his victims.

CASE CLOSED

When investigating a crime, detectives must exhaust every single line of inquiry in a bid to crack the case. Once they have done this, and all leads go cold, the case will remain open but go unattended as detectives concentrate on other crimes. If no new leads are forthcoming, the case will be closed and filed as a cold case.

Forlorn Hope

Many of the cold cases will never be looked at again, unless new evidence is found or a new witness comes forward. For the families of crime victims, especially in cases of homicide, this can be a frustrating and traumatic experience.

However, the development of modern forensic-science techniques gives them some hope. In certain cold cases, where there is sufficient evidence, it is possible to reexamine it using new scientific methods.

Collecting fingerprints from suspects is a key part of the criminal investigation process.

Scientists now regularly retest old case evidence using cutting-edge modern techniques.

Different Reasons, Same Outcome

There are many reasons that a cold case may be reopened. Sometimes, a convicted criminal will tell police what he or she knows about another unsolved crime, or a criminal will be linked to a historic homicide by fingerprint analysis or DNA testing. In other cases, it may be that modern techniques are able to unearth more clues from old evidence.

REAL-LIFE CASE

In 1988, Lisa Marie Kimmell was kidnapped and murdered while on a road trip to visit family in Montana. Her murder went unsolved until 2002, when detectives reexamined evidence using modern DNA testing. A DNA profile of the killer was made, and it matched that of a convicted felon named Dale Wayne Eaton. This new evidence allowed prosecutors to convict Eaton of Lisa Marie's murder.

11

CHAPTER TWO
THE FORENSIC TOOLBOX

Over the last 30 years, many forensic-science techniques have been advanced, perfected, or invented, allowing police to reexamine cold cases with new eyes. These techniques vary, but they all require a good knowledge of biology, physics, and chemistry.

Bloodstain Analysis

For many years, detectives working on cases of violent crimes, such as murders and attacks, have paid close attention to any blood-splatter patterns found at the crime scene. This is because the location and patterns of blood, such as on walls, floors, and clothing, can reveal a lot about exactly how the crime was committed. Today, bloodstain analysis is one of the essential forensic tools.

Samples of blood found at a crime scene are extracted from evidence and sent to a laboratory for testing.

Detailed Pictures

To help bloodstain analysis, crime scientists take detailed photographs and video footage of each crime scene. Once this is done, a bloodstain analyst will examine them to try to figure out what can be deduced from the blood patterns. This could be the entry angle of the weapon used in the attack, where the victim fell, whether the attacker was also injured, or the exact location of the crime.

Splatter Software

In the past, techniques for analyzing bloodstains were limited. Today, scientists understand a lot more about blood and why it makes the patterns it does when it hits a surface. Bloodstain analysts use computer software to create an accurate three-dimensional animation to show detectives how the blood ended up where it did. Since these animations are based on crime-scene photographs, they are of great use in cold cases.

BACK IN THE LAB

Bloodstain analysis is quite complicated, but the basic techniques used are easy to understand. For example, the length and width of a bloodstain pattern can reveal how far the blood fell before hitting a surface, and even the angle of entry of the weapon used in the attack.

Before testing blood, it must be carefully placed on sterile glass or plastic.

13

BALLISTICS

Another key forensic method regularly used by crime scientists on cold cases is ballistics. This is the scientific examination of firearms (guns), bullets, and gunpowder. Using scientific analysis, clues gained from firearms can be vital for solving violent crimes and robberies.

Firearms Laboratories

Gun crime is so widespread around the world that many police departments have their own firearms laboratories. These are places where forensic scientists can test weapons and examine them under microscopes.

Matching Guns

Ballistics experts also try to match recovered guns, for example, those found at a crime scene, with known attacks, robberies, or homicides. Ballistics analysis can tell crime scientists a lot about how a crime was committed.

Many US police forces have their own specialist ballistic test centers, where guns and bullets thought to be connected to unsolved crimes can be carefully examined for clues.

Cold Case Assistance

Ballistics is as important in solving cold cases as it is in regular crimes. Once a weapon has been found or recovered from a suspect, close analysis can help scientists to figure out exactly which crimes the weapon has been used to commit.

It may be that scratch marks inside the barrel of a gun link it to an unsolved crime. It is also possible that tiny traces of gunpowder residue found at a crime scene many years ago may also be found on or within the suspect's weapon.

"Dusting" bullets with a special powder can reveal fingerprints that may have previously been hidden.

CRACKED

One of the major ballistic discoveries of recent years is ballistic fingerprinting. This is the process of matching a bullet to a specific gun. When a gun is fired, microscopic scratch marks are left on both the bullet and the barrel of the firearm. These marks are unique to each bullet and weapon, making it a great way of linking a gun to an unsolved crime.

IMAGE ANALYSIS

For the best part of 100 years, crime-scene photographs have been a key part of the criminal investigation process. However, now that powerful computer programs allow crime scientists to examine images even more carefully, even the tiniest clues are not missed.

New Technology

Today, most photographs are taken digitally, so they can easily be stored and transferred between computers at the click of a mouse. It is also easy to digitize old photographs so they, too, can be stored on computers. In the past, detectives looking at crime-scene photos had to use a magnifying glass if they wanted to check minor details. Now, software programs make it possible to magnify images to hundreds of times their original size.

Crime-scene investigators may still use magnifying glasses to initially examine photos for trace evidence.

By reexamining crime-scene photos using modern software, scientists may find previously missed evidence.

Magnifying Clues

In order to reexamine old photos using computer software, scientists must first create an accurate digital copy of the original photo. This is done using a machine called a scanner. The scanner recreates the photo as a series of tiny dots and squares, called pixels. The smaller the dots and squares are, the more accurate the copy. By making a "high resolution" copy, with at least 300 tiny dots per inch (DPI), crime scientists can zoom in on tiny case-cracking details in the photo without it becoming blurred.

REAL-LIFE CASE

In the fall of 2011, FBI investigators reexamined the unsolved case of Nicholas Loris, an 11-year-old boy who was found dead in 1987. For 15 years, police could not figure out the cause of his death, and they suspected his parents of murder. By using new image software to examine original case photographs, they were able to confirm that he was killed by a dog.

FORENSIC DOCUMENT ANALYSIS

It is not just old photographs that can be of use to cold-case investigators. Other documents, such as typed or handwritten letters, can also now be reexamined and analyzed using modern scientific techniques.

Fraudsters and Murderers

Investigators call this process forensic document analysis. It is used to prove the validity of key documents in criminal cases, and sometimes their origin. It is also used to detect forged documents, such as passports and drivers' licenses. In the past, it has been used to solve many fraud cases (for example, when someone tricked a person or company out of money) but is increasingly used in criminal cases, particularly those involving handwritten notes or letters left by criminals.

Tracing the origins of fake documents, such as passports, may help cold-case investigators to locate criminals.

The shape of letters, how smooth and dark the lines are, and the space between letters, words, and lines can provide clues about the author of the handwriting.

Handwriting analysis is not as obviously scientific as some other forensic techniques. When comparing examples of handwriting, document examiners look in detail not just at how words are written, but also at the space between them and the pen strokes used by the criminal. They also look at the way sentences are structured and the type of words used by the author.

It's a Match!

Handwriting analysis is a tricky science, but it has proved important to a number of cold cases. The terrorist known as the "Unabomber" was caught because his brother noticed that his handwriting was similar to that used by the terrorist in letters sent to the police.

Ruling Out Suspects

Handwriting analysis has also been used in the unsolved case of the Zodiac Killer (see page 9). Although the criminal behind the murders has never been found, several suspects have been ruled out following comparison of their handwriting with that of letters written by the Zodiac Killer.

TOXICOLOGY

Crime shows on television often make reference to the results of toxicology tests. These are tests used to determine whether the deceased had swallowed or injected something dangerous, such as drugs, alcohol, or poison, in the days or weeks leading up to his or her death.

Chemical Examination

Toxicology has come a long way in recent years. By studying the contents of someone's blood, urine, or stomach, it is possible to detect different types of drugs and poisons.

At the Autopsy

In homicide cases where the cause of death is unknown, an autopsy may be performed. This is a detailed forensic examination of the body. Samples of the deceased's blood, urine, and stomach contents are taken and held on file for later examination.

Food and drinks are often tested to find out whether poison played a part in the cause of death.

CRACKED

Drugs and poisons often change form once inside the body, so toxicology is a complicated process. To help them, toxicologists often use a machine called a spectrometer. This separates a blood or urine sample into its component chemical elements. If there is something suspicious in the sample, however small the amount, the spectrometer will find it.

Forensic scientists carrying out autopsies look for signs of drug or alcohol use.

Crucial Science

Today, toxicology is routinely used in homicide cases, but this has not always been the case. In cold cases, toxicology can offer rare and vital clues to the detectives handling the case. If samples of blood or human hair are kept in storage, they can be retested using the latest techniques. Traces of certain drugs and poisons, for example, remain in human hair for many months or years.

CHAPTER THREE

TAKE A SECOND LOOK

Over the years, many criminal investigations have ground to a halt because of a lack of evidence. Sometimes, though, the evidence is there but goes unnoticed. This is when taking a second look, sometimes years or decades later, can get results.

Reexamining Evidence

The police have to deal with so many cases that sometimes a crime with little clear evidence may be forgotten or go unattended for years. Then, out of the blue, they may get a tip-off that reignites the case and leads to an unlikely conviction.

The area where evidence is found is marked out—even the position itself can help explain how a crime may have been committed.

Applying Science

In cold cases, a conviction is still rare. Usually, if a cold case is going to be solved years after the crime took place, it will be by reexamining old evidence using modern forensic techniques.

To avoid contaminating evidence with fingerprints or traces of their own DNA, investigators are required to wear gloves and to use sterilized tools.

Hidden Clues

Using many of today's leading forensic techniques, crime scientists can find previously hidden clues in the tiniest pieces of evidence, from shreds of fabric and a few millimeters of cotton to what looks like specks of dust. In years gone by, it would have been impossible to see this evidence, let alone test it. Today, forensic scientists have the tools to take old evidence out of storage, reexamine it, and make breakthroughs.

REAL-LIFE CASE

In Kentucky in 1968, police found the dead body of a girl but were unable to identify her. In 1998, a detective contacted the family of Barbara Ann Hackmann Taylor, who had gone missing in 1967, suggesting that the mystery body could be hers. DNA tests then confirmed that the mystery girl was indeed Barbara Ann.

TRACE ANALYSIS

Today, scientists use incredibly powerful microscopes that allow them to look at things that are far too small to be seen by the human eye. These advances have been particularly important in the field of trace-evidence analysis.

Evidence of Contact

Trace evidence is evidence left at a crime scene when two or more objects come into contact with each other. Sometimes, the contact is big enough for detectives to see. For example, marks left by a ladder skidding across a stone floor, the flecks of paintwork removed when someone brushes against a wall, or a torn piece of fabric from a criminal's clothing are all easily seen. However, not all trace evidence is visible to the human eye. If the same evidence is examined using a microscope, it is possible to discover many new and important clues.

Under microscopic examination, even the impression left behind by a person's skin can be seen at a crime scene.

When a gun is fired, microscopic particles of gunpowder dust are released into the air. These often settle on nearby objects or clothing. To find them, trace analysts must use a scanning electron microscope. This powerful tool allows scientists to magnify objects up to 500,000 times. These objects may be too small for the human eye to see.

This scientist is searching a gun for trace evidence such as fingerprints and tiny specks of gunpowder.

Powerful Microscopes

It is now routine for crime scientists working on cold cases to reexamine original evidence using powerful microscopes. By doing this, they may find many new clues, from specks of gunshot residue and tiny spots of blood to hidden fingerprints and rubber from the sole of a criminal's shoes. While trace evidence itself may not lead to a conviction, it can give cold-case detectives vital new clues about where to concentrate their efforts.

WHAT A BODY CAN TELL US

When all other avenues have been pursued, and when a cold case demands it, detectives can ask to reexamine a body, even if it has been buried for years. This extreme course of action is not taken lightly, but can be the difference between cracking a case and letting it go unsolved.

Hidden Poison

There are many reasons why a body could be dug up and reexamined. For example, on original examination, a death may have been attributed to natural causes, but new evidence suggests that foul play could have been involved. With today's advanced toxicology tests, it is possible to discover tiny amounts of lethal poison in a body many years after death. If cold-case detectives suspect poisoning, they may have little alternative but to exhume a body from its grave.

In rare and unusual cases, police may ask the family's permission to exhume a body in order to carry out new forensic tests.

To examine the DNA of a dead body, tissue samples are taken and sent to the laboratory for analysis.

Positive Identification

The other main reason for exhuming a body is to try to identify it. There are many examples of homicide victims who have been buried, following rigorous but unsuccessful attempts to identify them. Identification of bodies is now much easier because of the development of accurate DNA tests (see chapter four). Thanks to DNA, more cold cases are being solved than ever before.

REAL-LIFE CASE

In 2001, Julia Lynn Turner was arrested for poisoning and killing her partner, Randy Thompson, using antifreeze. Her husband, Glynn Turner, had died of a heart attack six years earlier, so police decided to exhume his body and retest it using modern toxicology techniques. The tests found that Turner, too, had been poisoned using antifreeze.

CLUES IN CLOTHES

One of the greatest uses of modern trace analysis is for looking in detail at clothing worn by crime victims and criminal suspects. Using the same methods as those used to detect gunshot residue, crime scientists can find vital new clues that are hidden deep in the fibers of clothes.

Threads of Evidence

If you look at any type of clothing under a powerful microscope, you will see that it is made up of many individual threads of fabric woven together to make one garment. As tiny parts of these individual threads can come loose in contact, a criminal could unwittingly leave them on the body of a victim. By examining evidence under a microscope, crime scientists may find clothing fibers.

Microscopes allow crime scientists to look at things that are much too small for the naked human eye to see.

28

Blood found on clothing can be carefully analyzed, providing crime scientists with more clues.

In 1996, six-year-old beauty queen JonBenet Ramsay was found murdered in her parents' basement in Colarado, but her killer was never found. In 2010, police reopened the case. They used modern DNA testing techniques to try to uncover the identity of a man whose DNA was found in JonBenet's clothes and under her fingernails. A hair, with matching DNA, was also found on her clothing. If police manage to trace the man, the DNA link may solve the case.

Buried in the Weave

The fibers of clothing may hold other clues that can be used in a cold-case investigation. For example, tiny amounts of gunshot residue could be buried in the weave of a sweater, coat, or T-shirt. It is also possible that evidence of human hairs or skin flakes could be caught in the victim's or suspect's clothing. In some rare cases, crime scientists have also found microscopic spots of human blood on clothing fibers.

Footprints and shoe marks left at a crime scene can determine the size and weight of a suspect and the brand of sneakers he or she wears.

29

CHAPTER FOUR

THE IMPORTANCE OF DNA

The single greatest tool in the forensic toolbox is DNA profiling. This is the process of using human DNA to identify individuals. Since the first DNA profile was made in England in 1984, the technique has revolutionized crime science and led to countless cold cases being cracked.

DNA Explained

To understand the significance of DNA, we must first understand what it is and how it works. All living creatures pass on their features to their descendents using genes or traits. We get some of our genes from our mothers and some from our fathers. Crucially, everybody's genes are slightly different, though they may share some similarities with their parents.

Gene Genie

Every one of the 100 trillion cells that make up the human body contains our genes, collected together as DNA. Our DNA is like the body's instruction manual and identification kit rolled into one. It tells us how to grow, how to repair ourselves, even how to think. It also can explain just who we are.

Human DNA is grouped together in a unique "double helix" shape.

This is a cross section of a human liver. Each tiny cell that makes up the liver includes DNA.

Hidden Identity

Human DNA was discovered in the 1940s, so scientists are only now beginning to really know how it works. They understand enough, though, to realize that it is the most conclusive way to identify an individual. For crime scientists, finding human DNA at a crime scene is the first step towards finding and catching a criminal.

REAL-LIFE CASE

Many cold cases have been solved thanks to matching DNA discovered at a crime scene with that of a suspect. Altemio Sanchez, a serial killer who murdered three women and attacked 14 others over a 25-year period, was finally caught in 2007 after police matched his DNA to DNA samples found at eight different crime scenes.

DNA PROFILING

In 1984, a scientist working at a British university revealed a new way of cataloging human DNA. From this, he was able to create a test that could be used to make an accurate DNA profile of any individual. Today, DNA profiling is invaluable to crime scientists around the world.

DNA Samples

Because human DNA is found in every body cell, it can be found in a wide variety of substances. For example, DNA is present in blood, hair, skin, nails, and saliva.

DNA Everywhere

If a criminal comes into contact with his or her victim or other objects scattered around the crime scene, it is likely that he or she has left some traces of DNA.

Investigators take a small sample of evidence that may contain DNA and put it in a sterile container. It is then sent to a laboratory where it is tested.

Scientists use a machine called a centrifuge to extract DNA from samples in test tubes.

CRACKED

There are various methods of extracting DNA samples. One of the most advanced is mitochondrial DNA analysis. Unlike standard DNA analysis, which takes samples from liquids (saliva, blood, and sweat) and soft tissues (skin), mitochondrial analysis is used to make up DNA profiles using bones and teeth.

DNA Match

If someone is arrested during a criminal investigation, it is likely that a sample of his or her DNA will be taken so that it can be compared with any traces of DNA found at the crime scene. Many criminals have been convicted on the basis of a DNA-profile match. The technique has also allowed cold-case investigators to reexamine old evidence to see if any traces of DNA can be found. If so, it gives them a positive lead. All they have to do then is match the DNA with a suspect.

DNA DATABASES

In recent years it has become common for police to take DNA samples from suspects and convicted criminals. The DNA samples are then stored in a national DNA database, which can be used when DNA is found at a crime scene in the future.

CODIS

In the United States, the national DNA database is called the Combined DNA Index System (CODIS). It was established in 1994, and in 2010 held more than 8.7 million DNA profiles on file. When investigating crimes, detectives will regularly check DNA samples found at crime scenes against records held in the CODIS database. If a match is found, this is known as a "cold hit." Such cold hits often identify suspects. However, on their own, they are not a guarantee of guilt.

This printout of a DNA profile, or "genetic fingerprint," holds vital information about a person's identity.

Cold-Hit Success

The CODIS database is also useful for detectives investigating cold cases. When a cold case is reopened, evidence will be reexamined and cross-referenced with the database. Many historic cold cases have been solved this way. One of the most famous examples occurred in the United Kingdom, where a man was arrested in 2006 for sending false letters to the police in 1978 claiming to be the "Yorkshire Ripper" serial killer. While the real "ripper" was caught in 1981, the identity of the hoaxer came to light only when crime scientists reexamined the 1978 letters and found traces of his DNA.

REAL-LIFE CASE

In 2002, a petty criminal named Rodrigo Rodriguez Hernandez left a Michigan prison. Before he left, a DNA sample was taken. When his profile was added to the CODIS database, it matched samples found in an unsolved murder case from 1994. Hernandez was quickly rearrested and put on trial for homicide.

Crime scientists collect DNA samples by rubbing a cotton swab on the inside of the suspect's mouth.

FAMILY TIES

Sometimes it is impossible for crime scientists to find an exact match using DNA databases such as CODIS (see pages 34–35). However, all hope is not lost. It can be possible to trace a criminal by concentrating on "familial DNA." Familial DNA is the genetic traits shared by families.

Family Affair

Although everybody's DNA is unique, DNA of members of the same extended family will be similar. This is because a percentage of genes are passed down through generations. The DNA of brothers, sisters, and cousins, for example, will share similar traits.

Finding a Family Match

In cases where no exact DNA match can be found, crime scientists will search for a partial match or family match. If a family match can be found, it helps to narrow down their search.

DNA reports help police to trace family members of both the victim and the suspects when investigating a crime.

DNA analysts test samples to create accurate DNA profiles of suspected criminals.

BACK IN THE LAB

Long Process

When searching for familial DNA matches, crime scientists use a special piece of software that narrows down the search to a set of agreed genetic traits. What they are looking for are specific genes that are likely to be unique to the family of the criminal they are searching for. The first US criminal caught in this manner was Luis Jaimes-Tinajero, who was arrested in 2008 for breaking into cars. Police initially found no exact match, but noticed that DNA obtained from blood samples found at the scenes bore a similarity to the DNA records of Jaimes-Tinajero's brother.

The scientists who test DNA samples are known as DNA analysts. Their main task is to carefully examine all evidence to find if there is any DNA present. Then they must test it to make up a DNA profile, which can be entered into a DNA database such as CODIS or compared with other samples relevant to the investigation.

37

CRACKING THE CASE

There is no doubt that modern DNA profiling techniques have had a huge impact on the way crime scientists work. They have also helped solve some of the world's most famous cold cases. However, on its own, a DNA-profile match may still not be enough to convict a suspect.

More Evidence Needed

Even if a suspect's DNA is found at a crime scene, it is not necessarily proof of guilt. In some trials, suspects have successfully argued that their DNA had been present at the scene for another reason. Some have also argued that the DNA evidence has been tarnished or contaminated. This means that the DNA samples have not been kept properly or securely, and that there is a chance that they have either been mixed up or confused with other samples.

DNA evidence has helped police to catch thousands of criminals.

Some suspected criminals have argued in court that DNA evidence is not as accurate as people think.

DNA Doubts

Nobody knows exactly how accurate DNA evidence is. Scientists say that it is 99.9 percent accurate, but critics claim there are flaws in the system. They say that there is roughly a 1 in 100,000 chance that a DNA match will be wrong. While that is still a very small chance, it demonstrates that DNA profiling can never be entirely correct on every occasion. Despite the doubts of some, DNA profiling is easily the most accurate method of identification crime scientists have.

BACK IN THE LAB

Police are becoming increasingly worried about the possibility of "fake DNA" being left at crime scenes or given by suspects in blood tests. In 1992, one suspect—a doctor who was accused of attacking unconscious patients—tried to trick blood testers by inserting a tube full of another person's blood into his arm. The trick worked three times before police eventually found a DNA match.

CHAPTER FIVE
REWRITING HISTORY

Using modern forensic techniques to look at old cold cases can bring great results. However, it can also work to the advantage of those wrongly convicted of crimes they did not commit. DNA evidence, in particular, is helping to rewrite history.

Identifying the Unknown

Every year, millions of people around the world go missing. Some are never found, and their families suffer the agony of not knowing whether they are dead or alive. Every year, mysterious dead bodies are found, too, which police are unable to identify. Today, crime scientists and DNA analysts use DNA profiling to try to identify these unknown bodies.

Being able to visit the grave of a deceased relative after years of not knowing if they dead or alive is a healing process for many people.

Major Breakthroughs

On a number of occasions, crime scientists have been able to identify cold-case murder victims using mitochondrial DNA testing of their bones or teeth, many years after they died. The US government now funds a program at the University of Texas dedicated to matching the remains of unknown murder victims with known missing persons.

Mitochondrial DNA

Using bones and teeth to identify people is the cutting-edge technique that is being used to identify the remains of victims of the 9/11 attacks in New York. It is also being used to trace relatives of those killed in the holocaust during World War II.

Scientists have finally found the body of Richard III using DNA examination.

REAL-LIFE CASE

In July 2012, archaeologists in Leicester, England, began a search to finally crack a 500-year-old mystery. They believed they had finally discovered the location of the grave of King Richard III, who was killed in battle in 1485 but whose body was never found. In September 2012, they found a skeleton under a parking lot that they believe to be the former King of England.

GUILTY UNTIL PROVEN INNOCENT

Over the years, many people have gone to jail for crimes they did not commit. Today, these people have been given a chance to prove their innocence thanks to recent advances in forensic science.

Police Mistakes

In the years before thorough scientific testing was used by criminal investigators, detectives had to rely on witnesses and basic police work to prove that a suspect was guilty. While these methods were often good enough to convict real criminals, they sometimes led to innocent people going to jail. Before the use of forensic science, the only hopes these people had of proving their innocence were either showing that the police made mistakes or the rare discovery of new evidence.

Due to the accuracy of modern DNA tests, fewer innocent people are sent to jail. However, mistakes are still made.

Vastly improved technology and forensic testing techniques mean that scientists have a greater chance than ever before of solving and closing cold cases.

Case Reopened

Today, in the United States, people convicted before forensic tests came into use can appeal to a judge to have the evidence in their cases reexamined. If this appeal is granted, crime scientists will carefully examine all evidence using modern forensic tools. On a number of occasions, this kind of forensic reexamination has proved that they are innocent and that the police made mistakes. When this happens, what was thought to be a "solved" crime suddenly becomes a cold case, and police must reopen the investigation to try to find the culprit.

REAL-LIFE CASE

In 1979, Gary Dotson was convicted of attacking and kidnapping his girlfriend. He said he was innocent, but his girlfriend said he did it. In 1987, his former girlfriend admitted she had lied in court. In 1989, new DNA tests on original case evidence finally proved that Dotson was innocent. He was the first person in the United States to be cleared of a crime using DNA evidence.

43

SCIENCE MAKING A DIFFERENCE

In the last 30 years, crime science has undergone a major revolution. It has gone from being a small, underfunded area to becoming the backbone of modern police work. Crucially, it has also helped crack thousands of unsolved mysteries.

Old Cases

In the days before the forensic-science revolution, most cold cases were never solved. When all leads were exhausted, the investigation would quietly close. More often than not, the case files would be put in storage, never to be looked at again. Now, with the development of high-quality DNA testing, trace analysis, toxicology, and other forensic methods, many police forces have their own cold-case teams.

Forensic testing is time-consuming and intricate, but it can be the key to solving a cold case.

By shining an ultraviolet light on this plastic bottle, the crime scientist hopes to find fingerprints or other trace evidence.

Cold Cases

Despite the advances in crime science and the formation of cold-case teams, not all mysteries can be solved. Sometimes, there is little evidence to reexamine, or DNA testing is simply inconclusive. DNA can be matched only if the person is already a suspect or the government has the person's DNA on file. Yet as crime science continues to evolve, and new techniques are invented, more criminals will be brought to justice for their crimes. As techniques improve and more criminals are caught the first time around, the number of cold cases will shrink.

BACK IN THE LAB

A new machine invented by a police scientist in England has breathed new life into fingerprinting, one of the oldest forensic science methods. The machine, nicknamed CERA, uses electricity and ceramic powder to reveal previously hidden fingerprints on metal surfaces, such as bullets and guns. Its inventor hopes it will help solve cold cases that have, until now, proven hard to crack.

GLOSSARY

advent start

analysis the careful study of something

antifreeze a substance used to defrost ice from car windows and to keep car engines from freezing in cold conditions

autopsy the examination of a dead body to figure out the cause of death and other details relevant to a criminal investigation

comparison differences and similarities between things

DNA short for deoxyribonucleic acid, the unique code inside every human body cell that controls every element of how we look

evidence material collected after a crime that can be used to identify the person who committed it

exhume to dig up a grave to take the body out of the ground

FBI short for Federal Bureau of Investigation, a government agency belonging to the United States Department of Justice

felon a criminal

fraction the amount of something

fragment a small piece of something

forensic the detailed study of a particular subject, such as science, for use in a court of law

forensic techniques the scientific methods used for collecting evidence in criminal cases

genes the traits and physical features passed down from parents to their children

homicide murder

laboratory any place where scientific testing takes place

lethal deadly

magnifying using tools or equipment to look at very small things

microscope piece of equipment used by scientists to look at incredibly small things

microscopic something that can be seen only with the aid of a microscope

murder to kill someone

notorious well-known

poison a harmful substance

residue a very small amount of something (for example, gunpowder)

serial killer somebody who murders a number of different people

software program something on a computer designed to do a specific task

toxicology science of working out what substances someone has taken, or been given, using laboratory testing

trace a very small amount

trace evidence marks or other evidence left when two or more objects come into contact with each other

traumatic very upsetting

unique one of a kind

unwittingly accidentally, without knowing

visible something that can be seen

witnesses people who have seen, or "witnessed," a crime

FOR MORE INFORMATION

BOOKS

Frith, Alex. *Forensic Science*. Tulsa, OK: EDC Publishing, 2007.

Gifford, Clive. *Crimebusters: How Science Fights Crime*. Oxford, UK: Oxford University Press, 2007.

Morrison, Yvonne. *The DNA Gave it Away! Teens Solve Crime*. New York, NY: Children's Press, 2008.

Rollins, Barbara B. *Fingerprint Evidence*. Mankato, MN: Capstone Press, 2004.

WEBSITES

Read the Civil Rights Cold Case Project website and discover attempts by the FBI and investigative journalists to try to solve famous cold cases from the civil rights struggle at:
www.coldcases.org

If you are still a little unsure about how DNA and genes work, find help at:
www.meddlingkids.org/2011/07/evolution-explained-for-kids-dna-and-traits

Read more about the methods of fingerprinting at:
www.science.howstuffworks.com/fingerprinting.htm

INDEX